LITTLE BIOGRAPHIES OF BIG PEOPLE

JIM HENSON

By Joan Stoltman

Gareth Stevens
PUBLISHING

Please visit our website, www.garethstevens.com. For a free color catalog of all our high-quality books, call toll free 1-800-542-2595 or fax 1-877-542-2596.

Library of Congress Cataloging-in-Publication Data
Names: Stoltman, Joan, author.
Title: Jim Henson / Joan Stoltman.
Description: New York : Gareth Stevens Publishing, [2019] | Series: Little biographies of big people | Includes index.
Identifiers: LCCN 2018003839| ISBN 9781538218471 (library bound) | ISBN 9781538218495 (pbk.) | ISBN 9781538218501 (6 pack)
Subjects: LCSH: Henson, Jim—Juvenile literature. | Television producers and directors—United States—Biography—Juvenile literature. | Puppeteers—United States—Biography—Juvenile literature. | Sesame Street (Television program)—Juvenile literature. | Muppet show (Television program)—Juvenile literature.
Classification: LCC PN1982.H46 S76 2018 | DDC 791.5/3092 [B] —dc23
LC record available at https://lccn.loc.gov/2018003839

Published in 2019 by
Gareth Stevens Publishing
111 East 14th Street, Suite 349
New York, NY 10003

Designer: Sarah Liddell
Editor: Kate Mikoley

Photo credits: series art Yulia Glam/Shutterstock.com; Cover, pp. 1, 5 Nancy R. Schiff/Contributor/Archive Photos/Getty Images; p. 7 Bettmann/Contributor/Bettmann/Getty Images; p. 9 Mark Wilson/Staff/Getty Images News/Getty Images; p. 11 David Attie/Contributor/Michael Ochs Archives/Getty Images; p. 13 Nancy Moran/Contributor/Sygma/Getty Images; p. 15 Hulton Archive/Handout/Moviepix/Getty Images; p. 17 Frederick M. Brown/Stringer/Getty Images Entertainment/Getty Images; p. 19 Ted Thai/Contributor/The LIFE Picture Collection/Getty Images; p. 19 (inset) Time & Life Pictures/Contributor/The LIFE Picture Collection/Getty Images; p. 21 Colin McConnell/Contributor/Toronto Star/Getty Images.

Printed in the United States of America

CPSIA compliance information: Batch #CS18GS: For further information contact Gareth Stevens, New York, New York at 1-800-542-2595.

CONTENTS

Boldface words appear in the glossary.

A Happy Childhood

Jim Henson was born in 1936 in Mississippi. He loved **comedy** and trying out all kinds of art. Jim spent lots of time with his grandmother. She was an artist and taught Jim how to paint, draw, and sew.

The Spark of Creation

In fifth grade, Jim's family moved to Maryland. He loved art and TV. He **created** sets for school plays and drew a cartoon for his high school's yearbook. In high school, he also began creating **puppets** for a TV show.

"When I was young, my **ambition** was to be one of the people who made a difference in this world."

—Jim Henson

Success as a Young Adult

Jim soon got his own TV show, Sam and Friends. The show was only 5 minutes long. It featured an early Kermit the Frog! Jim worked on the show with Jane Nebel, who he later married. Together, they founded the Jim Henson Company.

Sesame Street

Hearing how creative Jim was, a group called the Children's Television Workshop asked him to help create a new children's show. The show, Sesame Street, began in 1969. It was so loved, it ran in more than 80 countries and in 14 languages!

Muppets!

In 1976, *The Muppet Show* began.

"Muppet" was a word Jim came up with that brought together the words "puppet" and "**marionette**."

The show became one of the most successful TV shows of all time.

It showed in over 100 countries!

Creating and Teaching

Jim used puppets in movies and TV shows to spread important messages. *Fraggle Rock* began in 1983. It taught children about **diversity** and peace. Before it showed in another country, it was sometimes reworked to make sense for that **culture**!

Puppets with Feelings

Some puppets are made out of wood. But when making Kermit, Jim had the idea to use cloth instead. Cloth made it easier to move the puppets' faces. This way, the puppets could make faces that showed humanlike feelings.

A Different Kind of Boss

Jim saw failing as a way to learn how to do better. He was a **calm,** fun leader. He loved laughing and making good work. Jim was a great listener and loved to hear other people's ideas and thoughts.

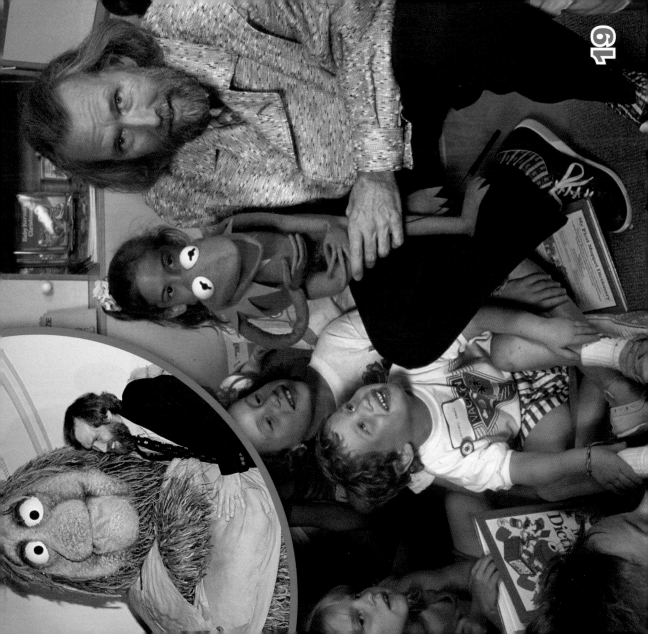

Remembering Jim

Jim died in 1990. He lives on through the magical worlds and more than 2,000 puppets he created. His creations and ideas changed TV and movie-making forever. But his life's work isn't just about puppets. Jim Henson is proof that kindness and respect can bring success!

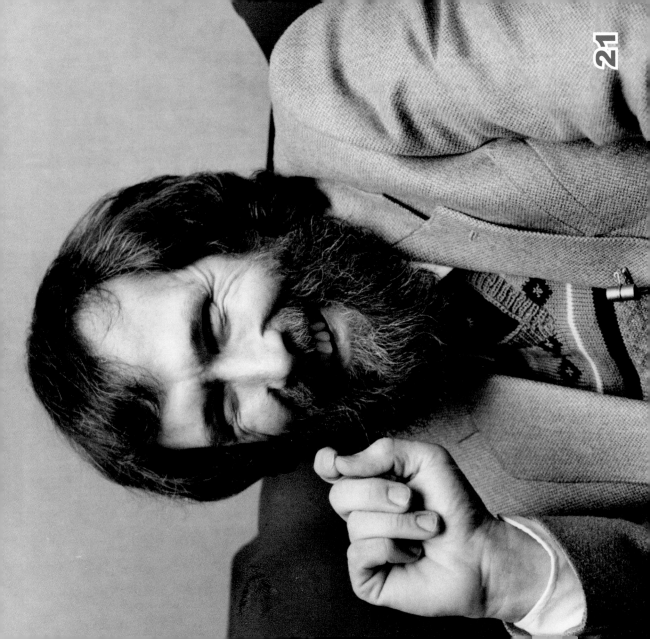

GLOSSARY

ambition: something that a person hopes to do

calm: not angry, upset, or excited

comedy: things that are done or said to make people laugh

create: to make something new

culture: a group of people that has their own beliefs and ways of life

diversity: the state of having people in a group who are different races or cultures

marionette: a puppet that is moved by pulling strings or wires that are connected to its body

puppet: a doll that is moved by putting your hand inside it or by pulling strings or wires

FOR MORE INFORMATION

BOOKS

Meltzer, Brad. *I Am Jim Henson.* New York, NY: Dial Books for Young Readers, 2017.

Reynolds, Toby. *Making Puppets.* New York, NY: Windmill Books, 2016.

Shemin, Craig. *The Muppets Character Encyclopedia.* New York, NY: DK Publishing, 2014.

WEBSITES

Jim Henson - Mini Biography
www.biography.com/video/jim-henson-mini-biography-50003523550
Watch this short video all about Jim!

Jim Henson Timeline
www.jimhensonlegacy.org/jim-henson/time-line
Check out this timeline and discover many of Jim's most important moments!

Who Was Jim Henson?
wonderopolis.org/wonder/who-was-jim-henson
This website includes a biography, quotes, and activities to help you learn more about Jim Henson.

INDEX